Final 9/11/18

DEMOCRATS OVERTAXED ALL OF US SINCE 1951

DEMOCRATS OVERTAXED ALL OF US SINCE 1951

DEMOCRATS

Truman   Obama   Biden   Schumer   Pelosi

OVERTAXED

All of us since 1951

By

Great Grandpa Kelly

Korean War Veteran, U. S. Army

DEMOCRATS OVERTAXED ALL OF US SINCE 1951

Introduction:

I served in the U.S. Army during the Korean War, 1951 - 1953.

At that time, and totally unknown to me, President Harry S. Truman, a Democrat, launched TAX THE RICH.

1. He raised the Federal Corporate Income Tax from 42% to 52%.

2. He raised the Top Federal Personal Income Tax from 91% to 92%.

The Democrat added an Excess Profits Tax of 30% for 1951 - 1953.

TAX THE RICH Truman could take up to 97% of the profits from America's War-Winning manufacturers.

Democrats screwed every working person since 1951.

DEMOCRATS OVERTAXED ALL OF US SINCE 1951

WHY I WROTE THIS BOOK

I am nearing age 90, heading a family of more than two dozen members. My wife and I were blessed with five children, many grandchildren, and the next generation is off to a great beginning.

You will read how my life's works improved your lives. I also have unique knowledge that must be shared to improve the lives of all of the peoples of Planet Earth.   Signed   Great Grandpa Kelly

TAX THE RICH Democrats raised the price of a Levittown "starter" house from $7,999 in 1947 to over $425,000 in 2018.

TAX THE RICH Democrats increased our National Debt from 252 Trillion to 21,456 Trillion in the same time period.

Do the math: Democrats multiplied our debt to 85 times the value it was before they launched TAX THE RICH.

TAX THE RICH Democrats made borrowing PROFITABLE to the very rich, and screwed the rest of us.

TAX THE RICH Democrats are loaded with America haters who will do all in their power to hurt our elected leader, President Donald J. Trump.

Educate voters in your family about Democrats evil habits. Or they will undo all the good President Trump is doing.

DEMOCRATS OVERTAXED ALL OF US SINCE 1951

In memory of
Charles Krauthammer,
a rare courageous journalist,
whose final column
is reprinted below.

"The pursuit of truth and right ideas through honest debate and rigorous argument is a noble undertaking."

DEMOCRATS OVERTAXED ALL OF US SINCE 1951

INDEX

Page #   Content

3………………………… Title

4…………………………. Introduction

5………………………….. Why I wrote this book

6…………………………. Dedication

7……………………………… Index

8…………………………..Thank you President Trump

10……………………….About the author

20   CHAPTER 1. ……..Truth lays a strong foundation

32   CHAPTER 2……….Tax cuts

39   CHAPTER 3……….Rethinking the tax code

47   CHAPTER 4 ……….Drain the Swamp

48   CHAPTER 5………..Jobs

51   CHAPTER 6………..Immigration

54   CHAPTER 7………..Helping hand tax shelters

56   ……….End notes

Copyright 2018 by J. T. Kelly
ISBN-13: 978-1727160789
ISBN-10:1727160789

DEMOCRATS OVERTAXED ALL OF US SINCE 1951

Thank you President Trump

for making America greater every day.

I'm here to help you win three more elections.

2018   2020   2022

My four most powerful tools are:

Age, Knowledge, Experience and Truth.

When voters learn how many tens of thousands of dollars Democrats have cost them in higher housing costs, higher automobile costs, higher college costs, higher medical costs and endless price increases since 1951, the SMART ONES will become Republican Voters.

My life's works have improved the lives of almost everyone on Planet Earth for 65 years.

(I'm almost 90. This may be my last noble undertaking.)

Great Grandpa Kelly
Korean War Vet U.S. Army

DEMOCRATS OVERTAXED ALL OF US SINCE 1951

President Trump has asked for input on key topics. Several topics are chapter headings in this book.

I am providing experienced views he might like.

To gain credibility with voters, I must tell you who I am, what I have done, how my life's works have improved your lives and how long I have been The Middle-Class Tax Advocate!

L will also outline how a SMART TAX CODE can correct 67 years of Democrats bad judgements.

Please allow me to introduce myself and itemize a few of my contributions to you, America, and to the World.

I have helped millions, everywhere, since 1953.

Great Grandpa Kelly

DEMOCRATS OVERTAXED ALL OF US SINCE 1951

About the author:

My fellow humans: I have improved your lives in several surprising ways, depending upon your age and citizenship. Nearly every age group in every Nation benefited from my life's works.

Americans benefited the most.

Born in 1929, I grew up in Queens County, NY, during the Great Depression. Queens County is home to LaGuardia Airport and JFK Airport.

I met Mayor LaGuardia in 1938 at age nine because  my father worked for him. The Mayor was using eminent domain to buy the land for what today is the John F. Kennedy International Airport, Van Wyck Expressway and the Belt Parkway.

I walked acres of sand after the area suffered extreme damage from the 1938 hurricane nicknamed "The Long Island Express."

My late father settled claims against New York City for many years. His 1940s job title was "Chief Clerk, Bureau of Tax Assessors, Division of Claims."

With only a 6th Grade education, Dad proved that a common person can rise on their skills by applying themselves and doing their best every day.

In about 1995 Mayor Rudy Giuliani personally advised me that the department my father once headed was no longer needed and had been closed.

Former Mayor Rudolf Giuliani is now an attorney for President Trump. I have admired him for decades.

DEMOCRATS OVERTAXED ALL OF US SINCE 1951

My actions that improved so many lives evolved naturally as I adjusted to war, changing employment opportunities, tax laws, family health, my child's extreme illness, and God given insights that will be revealed.

On June 25, 1950, North Korea invaded South Korea. President Truman drafted me in January 1951 at my age 21.

I served in the U.S. Army during the Korean War, 1951 -1953. At the Armored School, Fort Knox, KY, my training included that of a Tank Commander.

President Truman ordered Rotation of Troops from the War Zone. The Army wisely used my pre-war experience at Union Carbide International, and ordered me to set up a Separation and Replacement Center at Camp Atterbury, Indiana.

My rank was the Army's lowest, Private, E-2.

Korean War Veterans arrived in groups of 40 to 185 at any hour of the day on any day of the week. Our mission was simple: Feed them on arrival, regardless of the hour. Then get those war weary men haircuts, showers and shaves, two new uniforms, 30 days leave orders, 60 days' pay in cash and have them homeward bound within 24 hours of arrival. I was honored to work to serve their needs.

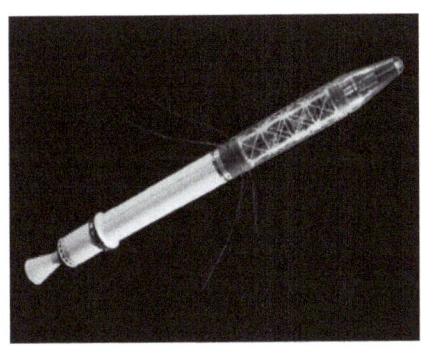

Upon release, I became an inventor for Union Carbide in their Speedway, Indiana, Linde Air Products laboratory. There, in 1953, I set up the first link between Corporate America's oxygen delivery skills and our first rocket launching site, Cape Canaveral. Americas' first orbital rocket, Explorer 1, launched two years later, in 1955. Details in End notes.

DEMOCRATS OVERTAXED ALL OF US SINCE 1951

The Lab team also launched Jet passenger travel. One Linde Air Products invention was key. Tungsten carbide is the hardest metal on earth. Only diamonds are harder. Tungsten carbide plating was applied to Jet engine impeller blades via a 6,300 degrees Fahrenheit oxy-acetylene cannon.

The process was called Flame-Plating. In time, as of my last contact with a Linde sales engineer in 1976, Linde Air Products division of Union Carbide had built 24 Flame-Plating plants in the free world. Flame-Plating the compressor blades with tungsten carbide allowed Jet Engines to endure the wear and stress of extended flying hours.

In 1953, as a young Union Carbide Inventor, I advised installing a Flame-Plating plant near the Pratt &Whitney factory to save shipping expenses. Details in End notes.

On July 15, 1954 this Boeing Jet Liner was the first American aircraft to enter commercial passenger service. Four Pratt & Whitney jet engines each provided 10,000 pounds of thrust.

It was later labeled a 707 and immortalized in John Denver's song and Peter, Paul and Marys' recording, "I'm Leaving on a Jet Plane."
In 2017 over 160,000 passengers left JFK on Jet Planes daily.

DEMOCRATS OVERTAXED ALL OF US SINCE 1951

My wife and I had a flight on the Rolls Royce powered Concorde years later. The pilot stated, "We are in orbit at 60,000 feet, flying at twice the speed of sound. Tell your grandchildren that you saw for yourselves that the Earth is round." We both looked out the windows and saw the curvature.

The world-famous Indianapolis Motor Speedway was across the street from the Linde Air Products factory and laboratory where I worked for five years.

Sadly, my inventers job left Indiana for parts unknown in 1958 due to President Harry Truman's TAX THE RICH policy.

Some years later I was selling Federal and State Tax and Business Law Reports and the computer-based tax service, COMPUTAX, for the Commerce Clearing House. (Now Wolters Kluwer N.V.) My initial sales territory was two blocks by two blocks on the south face of Grand Central Terminal in New York City.

My customers included Admiral Arleigh Burke, who had served as Presidents Eisenhower and Kennedy's Chief of Naval Operations. Admiral Burke reshaped the U.S. Navy. Today, the Arleigh Burke class of Guided Missile Destroyers

are currently the backbone of the United States Navy. They allowed President Trump to attack Syrian Poison Gas facilities in April, 2017, and again, in the Spring of 2018.

DEMOCRATS OVERTAXED ALL OF US SINCE 1951

My large customer base included the private accounting office's for both the Kennedy and Rockefeller families, CPAs for rock stars like Beatle George Harrison, movie stars including Kathern Hepburn, and hundreds of other individuals, partnerships, proprietorships and corporations. Several of Wall Street's largest law firms and financial institutions like J.P. Morgan-CHASE became my customers.

On April 10, 1972 I conferred with the Honorable James J. Delaney, Chairman of the House Rules Committee. Later that day I proposed the Individual Retirement Account, IRA, concept to Wilbur Mills, Chairman of the House Ways and Means Committee.

Chairman Mills said, "I wish I'd thought of that!"

President Gerald R. Ford of Michigan created IRA's when he signed the ERISA law on Labor Day 1974. I immediately sought recognition for my proposal. Unfortunately, Chairman Mills had been caught cavorting in the Washington Tidal Pool with the Argentine Stripper Fanny Fox. He resigned in disgrace.

The Committee refused to acknowledge my role in helping millions of Americans retire with comfort and security, claiming it was their idea all along.

Those Democrats betrayed me. I changed party.

DEMOCRATS OVERTAXED ALL OF US SINCE 1951

Here is an illustration of what my suggestion to Chairman Mills has done for you and every thinking American.

This is a list of the worlds' 10 most valuable brands.

RANK	NAME	VALUE	
10	TARGET	13.67	BILLIONS
9	LOWE'S	14.02	BILLIONS
8	WALGREENS	15.54	BILLIONS
7	JD.COM	19.62	BILLIONS
6	CVS	20.6	BILLIONS
5	IKEA	24.35	BILLIONS
4	HOME DEPOT	33.74	BILLIONS
3	ALIBABA	54.92	BILLIONS
2	WALMART	61.48	BILLIONS
1	AMAZON	150.81	BILLIONS
	TOTAL	408.75	BILLIONS

The total value of the top ten businesses in the world is $408.75 BILLIONS.

That is only $0.408 TRILLION

The current value of all IRAs and 401s is over $12 Trillion.

The 12 trillion divided by 0.4 trillion equals 30.

DEMOCRATS OVERTAXED ALL OF US SINCE 1951

You, my fellow Americans, have accumulated tax free retirement savings equal to 30 times the value of the ten largest businesses in the world. **Take a bow.**

Please buy extra copies to advise your loved ones of how they can help shape the world as this old man has done.

DEMOCRATS OVERTAXED ALL OF US SINCE 1951

In time I learned that two single people got twice the tax-free gain on the sale of their home as a married couple. I attacked it as un unfair "Marriage Tax" in a 1968 book, now out of print.

Many copies were sent to members of Congress for years. In time one copy may have reached Leon Panetta, President Clinton's Chief of Staff.

President Bill Clinton, in 1997, raised the tax-free gain on the sale of a home from $125,000 per couple to $250,000 per person, and $500,000 per couple.

That tax break was originally a once in a lifetime event. President Clinton broadened it and made it available as a recurring joy.

Congress should rethink allowing some tax payers two, three, four or more $500,000 tax free gains.

That "only the super-rich" advantage is unfair to America's overtaxed working families.

I pray President Trump will advocate fairness.

DEMOCRATS OVERTAXED ALL OF US SINCE 1951

In 2013 I learned that Albert Einstein did not understand the tax code. Most people of the world believe that Einstein was one of the smartest men in history.

I concluded there was a flaw in the law and starting looking for it. When you learn how I found it, you may agree I was the beneficiary of a Minor Miracle.

After our short 1951 wartime honeymoon, I bought a New York Times at the NYC bus terminal. Next day I returned to my Indiana army base. My mother-in-law used that newspaper to wrap wedding gifts and other material.

Decades later, after her passing, that aged newspaper gave me the key clue story of how corporations responded to Truman's TAX THE RICH policy. Details later in this book.

May I ask you a question?
Have weather reports from satellites helped you avoid disasters?
Are you one of the millions of world citizens flying on Jet Airliners?
Do you own part of the $12,300,000,000,000 Pot of Gold in IRA's and 401K's? (That is $12.3 trillion -11 zeros- in retirement funds.)
Have you sold a home in retirement for your $500,000 tax free gain?
Have I helped you live better?

If you answered "Yes" to any question, please buy this book now, then tell ten smart people to do the same.

Read on to learn other ways you and your family can profit from my 80 plus years of asking questions and learning from thousands of persons I met only briefly.

Great Grandpa Kelly

DEMOCRATS OVERTAXED ALL OF US SINCE 1951

DEMOCRATS

Truman   Obama   Biden   Schumer   Pelosi

OVERTAXED

All of us since 1951

If re-elected, they promise they will overtax us again.

DEMOCRATS OVERTAXED ALL OF US SINCE 1951

CHAPTER 1. TRUTH LAYS A STRONG FOUNDATION

World War II ended on VJ-Day, September 2, 1945. People were dancing in the streets all over America and Europe.

Sixteen million American Military personal came home after five years of war. They needed meaningful lives, mates, houses, jobs and schools.

Many veterans had fought through years of battles, losing comrades and relatives daily.

For many couples, getting home was time to get busy and raise a family.

They launched the BABY BOOM.

National Goal: Replace the loses of a brutal war.

Many Veterans lived on the GI bill, with 52 weeks of $20 checks as their primary support.

My father, and millions of other adults, converted spare rooms into temporary living spaces for Veterans.

DEMOCRATS OVERTAXED ALL OF US SINCE 1951

Just a few miles east of JFK International Airport, in Queens County, N.Y., is Nassau County, New York.

There, a private builder, Levitt & Sons, created Levittown to fill the housing needs of Americas' War Veterans. The homes were built on private lots, with wrap around yards.

By 1947, Levittown became America's first suburban community.

An early home price was $7,990: The terms were $90. down and $50. per month mortgage.

Thousands of families found a place where they could become property owners instead of perpetual NYC renters.

DEMOCRATS OVERTAXED ALL OF US SINCE 1951

THEN OUR WORLD CHANGED

On September 25, 1950, North Korea invaded South Korea. Millions of Americans asked, "Where on Earth is Korea?"

President Harry S. Truman ordered American forces into battle to stop the world-wide spread of Communism.

I was drafted in January 1951, and joined the 28th Infantry Division at Camp Atterbury, Indiana. After basic training, I was assigned to The Armored School, at Fort Knox, KY, where I was trained as a Tank Commander. I used a tank of the type Patton had used winning WWII.

Tank training complete, I returned to Indiana and learned that my Division was headed for Europe, but I wasn't.

President Truman had ordered "Rotation" of those troops fighting in Korea since day one of the battle. Based upon my pre-war experience at Union Carbide International, I was ordered to set up a "Separation and Replacement Center" from scratch. My rank was the lowest in the Army: Private E-2.

My orders were simple. Feed them on arrival, regardless of the hour. Then get those weary warriors' haircuts, shaves, showers, two new uniforms, 30 days leave orders, 60 days' pay in cash and have them homeward bound within 24 hours of arrival.

I proudly served returning G.I.s in groups of 40 to 185 that arrived at any hour of the day or night on any day of the week.

DEMOCRATS OVERTAXED ALL OF US SINCE 1951

At that time, and totally unknown to me, President Harry S. Truman, a Democrat, launched TAX THE RICH.

1. He raised the Federal Corporate Income Tax from 42% to 52%.

2. He raised the Top Federal Personal Income Tax from 91% to 92%.

The Democrat added an Excess Profits Tax of 30% for 1951 - 1953.

Democrats screwed every working person since 1951.

We all know a picture is worth a thousand words, so, on the following pages, I will convert those 'Percentage' words to pictures.

Image A. 100 pennies.

Each penny represents 1% of the last dollar of profit earned by major American corporations, before taxes, in 1951, 1952 and 1953.

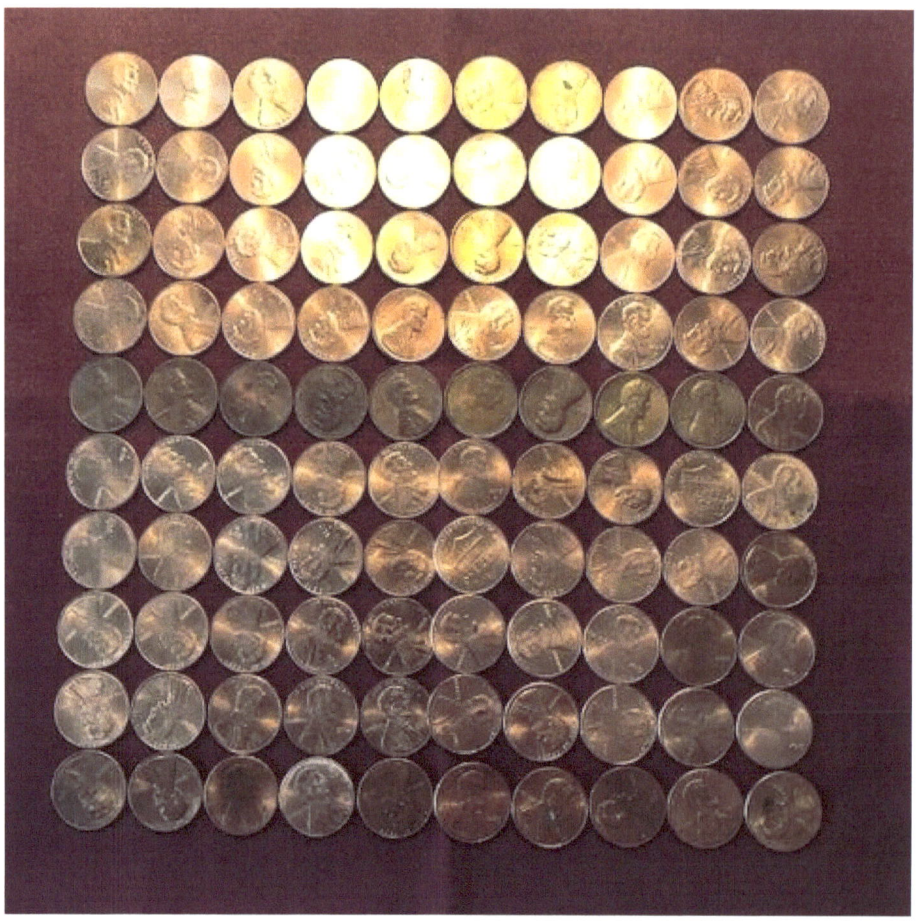

Theses 100 pennies = 100% 0f the wartime profits of America's largest War-Winning manufacturers.

DEMOCRATS OVERTAXED ALL OF US SINCE 1951

Image B. 52 pennies

Democratic President Harry S. Truman launched his TAX THE RICH laws in 1950, applicable to 1951, 1952 and 1953. The 52 pennies below illustrate the bite of Democrat Truman's Corporate Income Tax <u>on the last dollar of profit earned by the giant Corporations whose factories won World War II.</u>

Truman took 52 cents out of each dollar earned as a U.S. Corporate income tax.

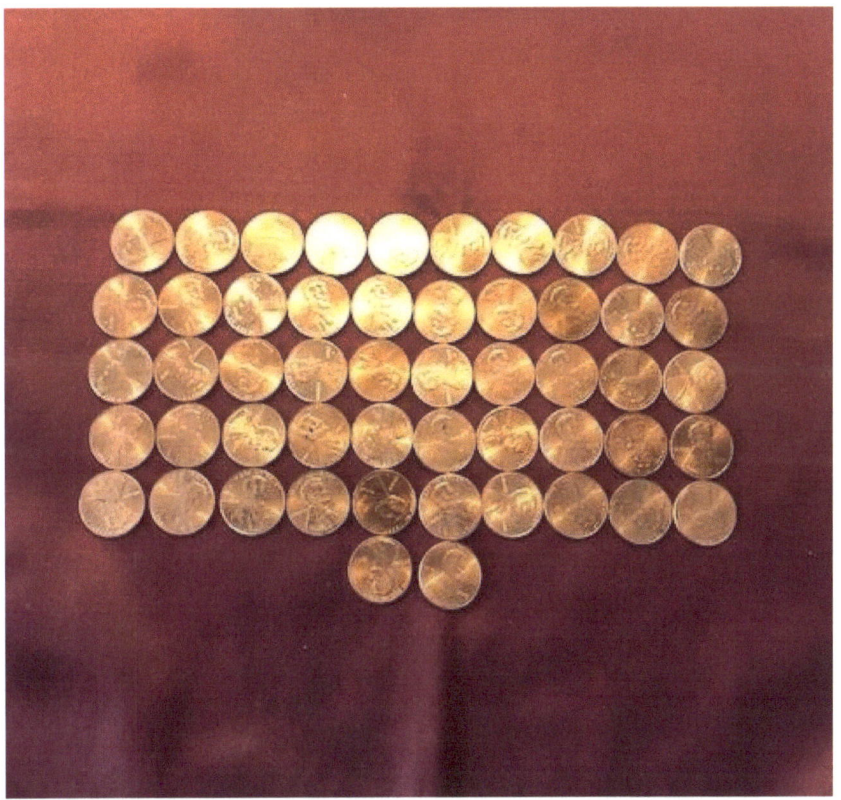

Next: Investors expect to earn dividends on their hard-earned money. This is how Truman's TAX THE RICH policy treated their 48 cents share if paid out in dividends.

DEMOCRATS OVERTAXED ALL OF US SINCE 1951

Image C. 48 pennies

48 cents left after 52% TAX THE RICH Corp. tax.

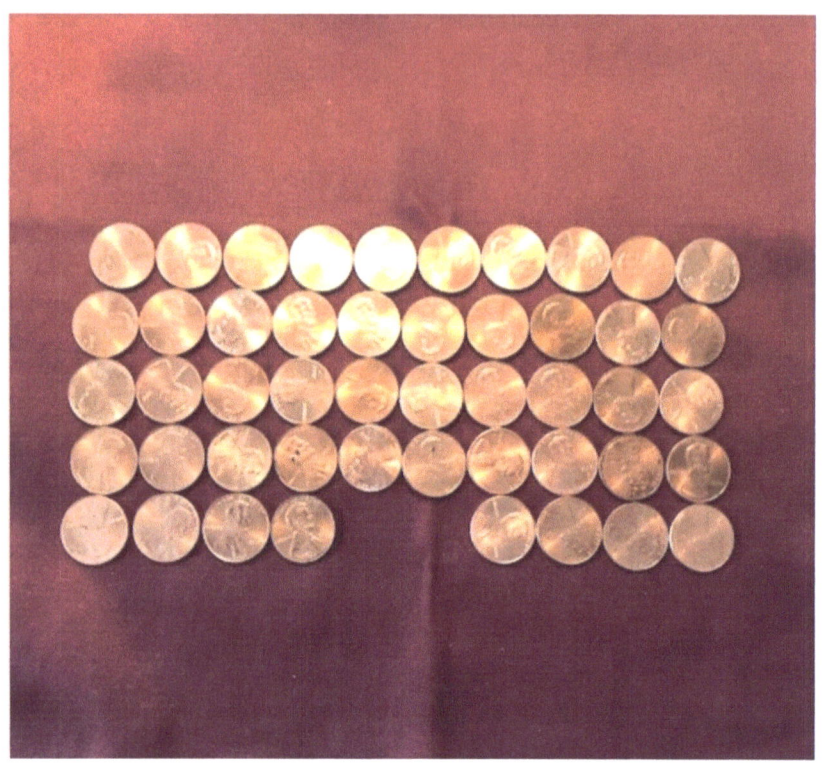

President Truman raised the top personal income tax rate from 91% to 92%.

The 48% left after taking 52% was taxed at Truman's 92% TAX THE RICH rate. Do the math: 92% of 48% is 44%.

Democrat Truman took 52 cents on the dollar, then 44 cents on the dollar.

Total: 96 cents on the dollar.

DEMOCRATS OVERTAXED ALL OF US SINCE 1951

Factory owners had only 4 cents on the dollar after two tax bites by DEMOCRAT Truman.

Image D: 4 pennies

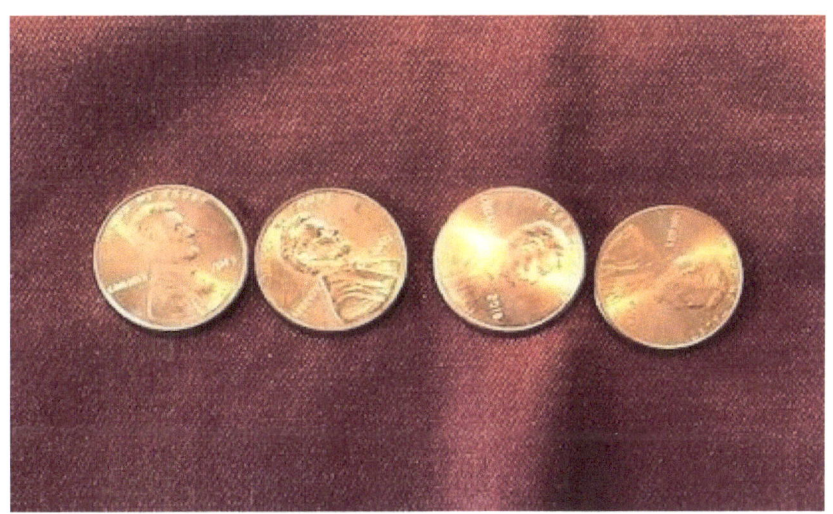

Those great companies did their War Winning Work for the USA. But most of their profit money was taken from them by President Truman's TAX THE RICH policy.

Do you think he was satisfied by taxing them almost into poverty?

No.

Not at all.

He wanted still more.

DEMOCRATS OVERTAXED ALL OF US SINCE 1951

Image E: 3 pennies

TAX THE RICH Truman took <u>52 cents on the dollar</u> in the U.S. Corporate Income Tax, and <u>44 cents more in the Maximum Personal Income Tax</u>, (52+44) = 96 cents out of every dollar that America's biggest manufactures earned in profits.

Democrat Harry Truman had suffered bankruptcy in his haberdashery business. Perhaps he held a grudge against successful and wealthy business owners.

After taking 96 cents on the dollar from them, he then applied a 30% Excess Profits Tax to their final 4 cents.

By taking just one more of their four pennies', Truman reduced them to only 3 cents on the dollar.

Recap on the next page.

DEMOCRATS OVERTAXED ALL OF US SINCE 1951

Recap of TAX THE RICH result.

Democrats TAX THE RICH policy took 52% as Corporate tax, then 92% of the 48%, or 44%, as Personal Income Tax, then 30% of the 4 cents, or 1% Excess Profits Tax, leaving the America's factory owners with only 3 cents on the dollar for their great work that won World War 2 for America.

DEMOCRATS OVERTAXED ALL OF US SINCE 1951

I repeat:

Democrats left only 3%, or 3 cents on the dollar, for the hard-working owners of Americas War-Wining factories.

Those people not only risked losing their life-long investments, but much, much, more.

Had Hitler had won WWII, the factory owners might have been enslaved if not assassinated.

Hitler could have done the same to millions of returning veterans and their families.

But Democratic President Harry S. Truman still took 97% of their profits anyway!

DISPICABLE!

Democrats currently running for election promise to bring back Harry S. Truman's TAX THE RICH tax rates.

DOUBLE DISPICABLE!

DEMOCRATS OVERTAXED ALL OF US SINCE 1951

Next, we look at America's leading industrialists' families. Their names were household names due to their decades, or centuries, of serving the people of America.

Dupont, who helped the Colonies win the War for Independence, also known as the Revolutionary War, must top any list.

Add Boeing, Chrysler, Firestone, Ford, Grumman, Kaiser, General Motors, Kellogg's, Pratt & Whitney, Proctor & Gamble, Standard Oil, and you get a glimpse of the families that America depended upon for reliable products to win any war.

Over 400,000 American military died in combat. Over 50 million people died worldwide during World War II.

Then some world leaders moved to improve the world.

The United Nations Organization was established at Lake Success, N.Y. on October 24, 1945. Goal: Reduce deaths by war. They started with 45-member states. Now there are 193. Many are currently at war with their neighbors.

John D. Rockefeller, an American investor, donated seven million dollars to buy the land in New York City to house the United Nations. The United States of America has been the largest financial supporter since it began.

Thank President Trump for getting many slackers to pay up.

DEMOCRATS OVERTAXED ALL OF US SINCE 1951

Chapter 2: TAX CUTS

Mr. President, when you were born in 1946, Americans were adjusting to their first full year of peace. Millions of former GI's were looking for work, housing and life mates.

By 1950 we were in the Korean War. You were only age four when I was drafted by President Truman at my age 21.

Borrowing has been going on since before Biblical times. The lender charged the borrower interest on his money from time immemorial. (i.e. Borrowing had always been costly to the borrower and profitable to the lender.) That was "economic reality."

When Democrat Truman started overtaxing everyone in 1951, he changed that "economic reality" that had existed since before Cleopatra.

DEMOCRAT TRUMAN

MADE MASSIVE BORROWING

'BY THE RICH'

PROFITABLE

'TO THE RICH'

DEMOCRATS HAVE SCREWED WORKING FAMILIES SINCE 1951.

DEMOCRATS OVERTAXED ALL OF US SINCE 1951

America's War Winning industrialists, owners of Dupont, Boeing, Chrysler, Firestone, Ford, Grumman, Kaiser, General Motors, Kellogg's, Pratt & Whitney, Proctor & Gamble, Union Carbide and Westinghouse and more were not stupid.

They knew Truman was out to get them as revenge for they being smarter and richer than he was.

They outsmarted Harry Truman by using his tax law.

This is the "Minor Miracle" news clip from our honeymoon that came to light 25 years after publication. By then I was providing tax return preparation by computer service for the Kennedys and Rockefellers and hundreds of others.

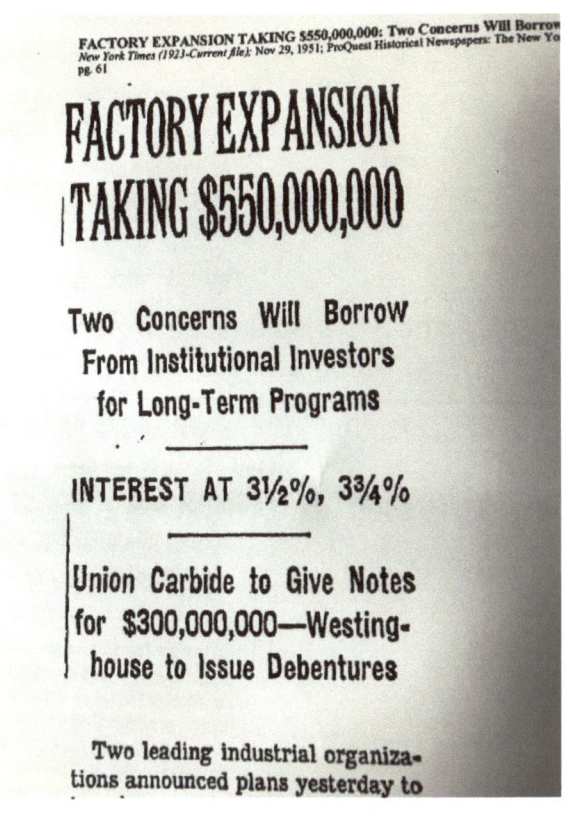

On November 29, 1951 the New York Times reported that Union Carbide and Westinghouse Electric borrowed $550,000,000 from Met Life and Prudential for a term of 100 years at 3 ½ and 3 ¾% interest. (I was then serving in the U.S. army during the Korean War.)

The 3 3/4% interest rate sounds cheap by standards since 1960. But I dug deeper. Ten years earlier, on Dec. 4, 1941, in the week before Pearl Harbor, the Treasury borrowed $1,000,000,000 (one billion) of new money for 25 and 30-year bonds.)

DEMOCRATS OVERTAXED ALL OF US SINCE 1951

Those 1967-1972 maturities paid 2 1/2% interest. Also that day, Treasury borrowed $500,000,000 (half a billion) in 10 & 15 years bonds paying 2%.

After the Met Life and Prudential loans, the U. S. Government had to equal or surpass the 3 3/4% interest.

Some of those 100-year loans may have been paid off in 25 years, but the higher interest rates remained for decades.

Federal Reserve Board Chairman Paul Volker pushed some rates over 15% during the Reagan administration. (1981-1989) His was a futile effort to stop inflation.

That proves that Democrat Truman's "TAX THE RICH" policy raised borrowing costs for every level of government, every national government, every business, every family and every college student since 1952!

TAX THE RICH also launched perpetual inflation which will be illustrated on the next page.

Mister President, you have recently shown displeasure as the Fed raised interest rates twice, and hinted at two more increases in 2018.

The bankers know that higher interest rates will slow down economic growth that you spurred by your tax cuts. They may want to stop your gains.

I will offer a solution in the next chapter.

DEMOCRATS OVERTAXED ALL OF US SINCE 1951

The Federal Reserve Bank was created by President Woodrow Wilson in 1913. They created the Consumer Price Index to gain insight into where money was flowing.

The chart below is the 105-year history of Consumer Price Index since the Federal Reserve was founded.

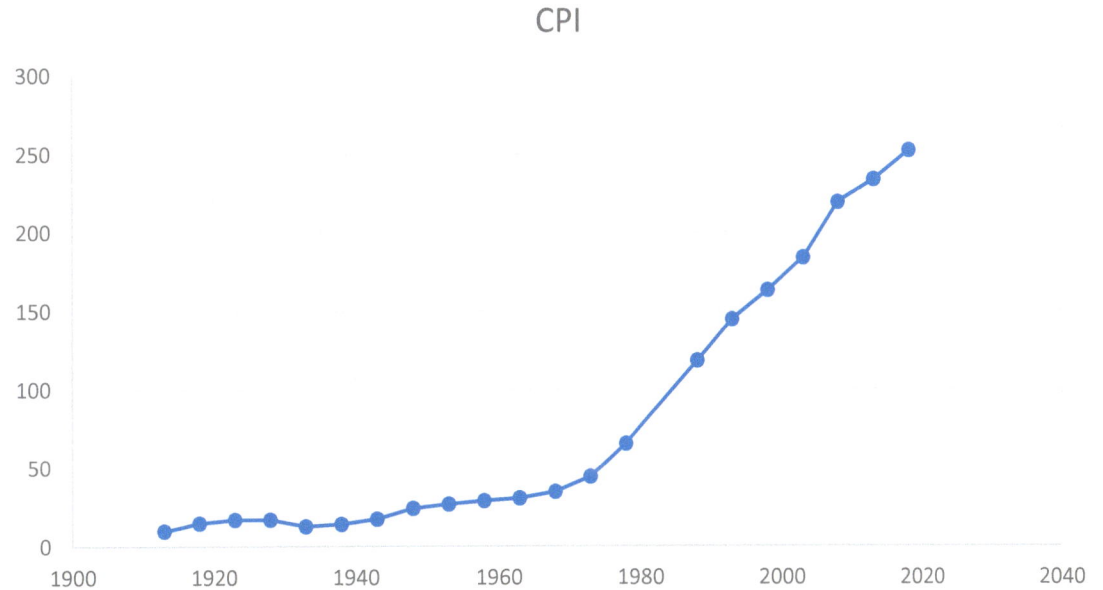

The chart above reveals that by the mid-1960s most financial planners had learned to use excessive borrowing to gain tax shelter for their clients. My most notorious customer, Leona Helmsley, "The Queen of Mean", owned the Empire State Building as a tax shelter.

Manny major properties are in tax shelter ownership.

In 1947 returning WW2 service members bought homes in several states for $90 down and $50 per month.

Every $1,000 borrowed was repaid for $250 interest.
As interest rates rose, the interest cost went to $500.
Then it went to $750.
Then it went to $1,000.

DEMOCRATS OVERTAXED ALL OF US SINCE 1951

When home mortgage interest rates rose to 14%, each $1,000 borrowed to buy a home cost families $3,265 interest on 30-year mortgages.

Mr. President, all of those high interest rate mortgages accumulated to become multi-billion-dollar tax deductions.

All those legal tax deductions are a major source of our growing National Debt.

Your decision to limit homeowner's tax deductions for real estate taxes and mortgage interest are steps in the right direction.

My experience included selling COMPUTAX Federal and State Income Tax Preparation by COMPUTER from 1971 to 1990.

I observed that people of wealth could make big investments with large Federal Income Tax <u>Deductions</u>. Those deductions were denied to average families**, putting many working families in higher tax brackets than millionaires and billionaires.**

That knowledge was part of my motive for proposing the IRA, or Individual Retirement Account plan, to Ways and Means in 1972.

The best way to solve the tax code is to throw away the Democrats "TAX THE RICH" internal revenue code completely.

Then take a look at the National Debt chart on the next page.

DEMOCRATS OVERTAXED ALL OF US SINCE 1951

The chart below left covers the 100-year history of the National Debt with the Federal Reserve in play. The graph below the chart illustrates growth of our debt since Democrats introduced their TAX THE RICH policy.

National Debt chart, 100 years 1918 - 2018

Date	Amount
8/28/2018	21,456,555,555,555.50
9/30/2008	10,024,724,896,912.40
9/30/1998	5,526,193,008,897.62
9/30/1988	2,602,337,712,041.16
9/30/1978	771,544,000,000.00
6/30/1968	347,578,406,425.88
6/30/1958	276,343,217,745.81
6/30/1948	252,292,246,512.99
6/30/1938	37,164,740,315.45
6/30/1928	17,604,293,201.43
7/1/1918	14,592,161,414.00

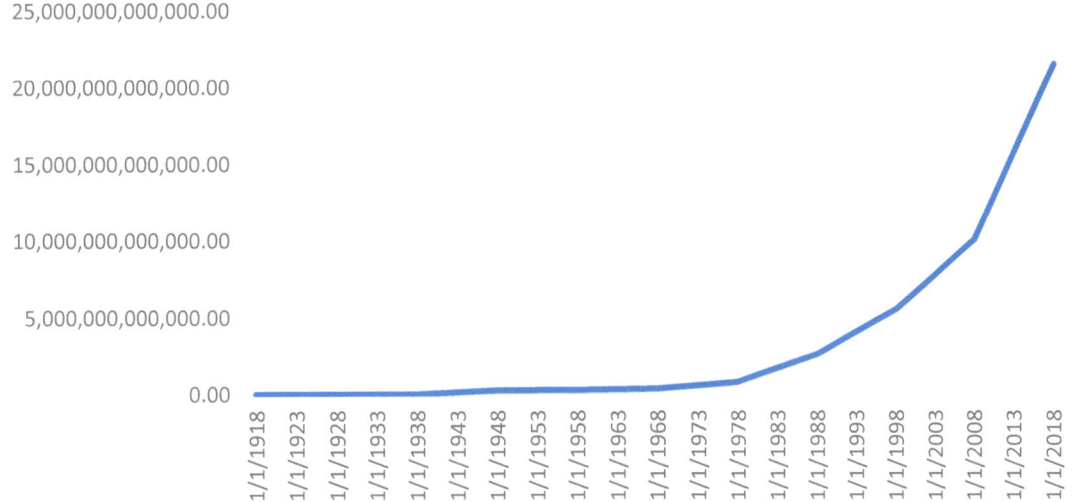

NATIONAL DEBT   100 YEARS 1918 - 2018

DEMOCRATS OVERTAXED ALL OF US SINCE 1951

Democrats made massive borrowing profitable to the very rich.

That created a 'Debt Preference' tax code.

The "unstoppable" growth of the U.S. National Debt is fed by the Democrats TAX THE RICH policy.

The "unstoppable" growth of the U.S. inflation is also fed by Democrats TAX THE RICH policy.

The "unstoppable" growth of the U.S. budget is also fed by Democrats TAX THE RICH policy.

The "unstoppable" growth of the budget deficit is also fed by Democrats TAX THE RICH policy.

Mr. President, anyone smarter than a 4th grader can see what must be done.

Money-Smart voters can act smart and DUMP every "TAX THE RICH" Democrat.

CHAPTER 3: RETHINKING THE TAX CODE:

Mister President, when a certified genius like Albert Einstein could not understand the tax code, we know we need to rethink the entire tax law.

America has had just one internal revenue code since 1914. It applies to both businesses and families. The deduction for interest on borrowed money was part of the law in 1914 when the Federal Corporate Income Tax rate was 1%.

Over the years, the tax code became so complex that even Albert Einstein did not understand it. We need to create new SMART TAX laws that serve the needs of both businesses and families.

We need a tax plan that Einstein and 8th graders would understand. It begins with a fresh new foundation of reasoning.

America's population is made up of two different and distinct organisms: Human beings and corporations.
Human beings each have a finite life span.
Corporations have infinite life spans.

The actions of President Truman revealed a very unfair competition for funds pitting decades old multimillion-dollar corporations against young newlywed couples in need of a starter home.

We must prioritize.
"Families" are every nation's greatest need.

America has too many homeless people. In addition, too many adults are living with parents after thirty-five years of age. Housing became prohibitively expensive for too many. There is a clear need for new thinking.

DEMOCRATS OVERTAXED ALL OF US SINCE 1951

Here is one line of new and different thinking.

In 1966 Democrats controlled the presidency and both houses of Congress. Two Columbia University professors and political activists Richard Cloward (1926–2001) and Frances Fox Piven (b. 1932), launched a plan to **bankrupt America by overloading our social services.**

Their goal was changing America to suit their vision of a world where the poor would not have to work for a living. They wanted a guaranteed annual wage without work requirements.

The married pair focused on forcing the Democratic Party to take federal action to help the poor. But first, they needed control of the Democratic Party. They planned to employ Community Organizers to ferment unrest and produce "Change."

Citizen Barack Obama worked as a Community Organizer to ferment unrest and produce "Change." It got him into the U. S. Senate.

In 2006, the debate was about President Bush raising the National debt limit to $9 trillion. Mr. Obama, then a freshman Senator from Illinois, published the following statement in the Congressional Record.

"Increasing America's debt weakens us domestically and internationally. Leadership means that "the buck stops here." Instead, Washington is shifting the burden of bad choices today onto the backs of our children and grandchildren.

"America has a debt problem and a failure of leadership. Americans deserve better.

"<u>I therefore intend to oppose the effort to increase America's debt limit.</u>" Barack Obama March 16, 2006.

Barack Obama held the Presidency from 2008 to 2016 and doubled the U.S. National Debt. It is currently $21.4 trillion.

Democrat Obama's words? Worthless!

DEMOCRATS OVERTAXED ALL OF US SINCE 1951

President Obama pushed us toward what the Federal Reserve Bank defined as the "Unsustainable" debt level. Was his motive Bankrupting us?

Compare the evil plan of one president to the noble work of a private corporation. Starting just after WWII in 1947, William Levitt and Sons sold homes in Levittown, N.Y. for **$7,990**. Levittown is in Nassau County, N.Y.

Today the Median price of a home in Nassau County is $540,000 according to the Multiple Listing Service of Long Island.

Do the math. $540,000 / $7,990 = 67.5.

Democrat's TAX THE RICH Inflation raised the price of a starter home by a multiple 0f 67.5. The $8,000 house of 1947 is now a 71-year-old 'fixer upper'. When updated, it costs about $500,000.
No wonder so many people are homeless.

Democrats definition of "Affordable Housing" is one where taxpayers pay for housing that other people live in either rent free or taxpayer subsidized.

I propose America adopt a new tax code that treats people as "human" beings, and corporations as "artificial" beings.

"Human" beings would not be forced to compete with "artificial" beings with superior financial power and unlimited life.

How can that be accomplished?

We now allow tax deductions on the use of borrowed money to both Human beings and Artificial beings.

That is the core of our problem since 1951.

DEMOCRATS OVERTAXED ALL OF US SINCE 1951

NEW PLAN. Why not give businesses an annual tax allowance for the use of their own capital? It will replace Truman's Debt Preference Tax Code with a new Equity Preference Tax Code.

By ending the 'business' vs 'families' competition for borrowing that has cost our nation billions in higher interest expense since 1951, you will reduce the revenue lost via the tax code.

We are looking at the national debt that accumulated over 240 years.

We must note the President Obama doubled the 232-year debt in his eight wasteful spending years. He even gave $150,000,000,000 (That is $150 Billion) to a foreign political enemy, Iraq.

History should classify Obama with Benedict Arnold.

Look back at two corporations borrowing $550,000,000 for 100 years. By taking income tax deductions for borrowed money for all of that time, they shifted their tax burden to other people who did not get tax deductions for that borrowing.

Humans will never have that advantage. So, we "humans" should strip that privilege from the 'artificial' non-human enterprises, corporations and businesses.

An EQUITY PREFERENCE TAX code can fix the flaws in current law.

Our "Income tax" law must stop helping the rich get richer.

But that is precisely what Truman and "TAX THE RICH" Democrats have done since 1951, a period of over 67 years up to 2018.

DEMOCRATS OVERTAXED ALL OF US SINCE 1951

What if businesses <u>could not</u> take tax deductions for interest on borrowed money, but instead could take annual deductions for the use of their own capital?

What if human families, and only human families, could take a tax deduction for interest on a mortgage?

To grasp the impact of reversing 100 years of tax law, understand that inflation will stop, prices will stabilize and working families will be able to plan on having their money safe and secure.

America's present **DEBT PREFERENCE TAX CODE** has increased the cost of living for every person on earth. It drove America to the present $21,400,000,000,000 National Debt. ($21.4 Trillion) (With 11 '0's)

A SMART TAX CODE

The proposed EQUITY PREFERENCE TAX RATE SCHEDULE would look something like this.
TAX FREE EARNINGS ALLOWED

First $25,000 invested, 10% or $2,500/year
Next $50,000 invested, 9% additional $4,500 "
Next $75,000 invested, 8% additional $6,000 "
Next $100,000 invested, 7% additional $7,000 "
Next $100,000 invested, 6% additional $6,000 "
Next $150,000 invested, 5% additional $7,500 "
That would allow to a small business with $75,000 capital investment to earn $7,000 tax free annually

A small business with $150,000 capital investment could earn $13,000 tax free annually A small business with $500,000 capital investment could earn $33,500 tax free annually. All additional invested capital: 4% tax free without limit.

(All of the above numbers could be reset higher or lower as needed.)

The Treasury Department would set tax rates on profits over these values.

DEMOCRATS OVERTAXED ALL OF US SINCE 1951

I favor 26 levels of tax rate brackets from 4% upwards in 1% increments. That would prevent the ten biggest corporations in each industry from exercising monopoly power in their industry.

A top rate of 25% might cover all the needs of Government. When the tax-free earnings are considered, the top total effective rate may be less than 20% for most businesses. That will spur investment, create jobs and produce shared prosperity.

Owners could borrow money, but they could not take any tax deduction for interest on those funds. That limit will protect the public interest by preventing high interest loan costs from impacting others.

Decades ago a prior owner of the Empire State Building was deeply in debt, with interest rates over 15%. He got huge tax deductions, and the taxpayers paid for much of his debt Interest.

No taxpayer would never be responsible for the debts of any other entity under this proposed EQUITY PREFERENCE TAX CODE.

IMPLEMENTATION: INSTANT OR GRADUAL?

If Congress adopts an EQUITY PREFERENCE TAX CODE, should it be adopted and enforced overnight? Or phased in over time?

My earliest big business experiences have been at Union Carbide International. After the U.S. Army, it was the Linde Air Products laboratory.

After TAX THE RICH law sent my inventors job overseas, I was employed selling law reports as diverse as US Tax and Securities, Aviation, Trade, British, Australian, Papua New Guinea tax law and 200 other legal subjects.

I suggest gradual adoption to give industries time to adapt.

DEMOCRATS OVERTAXED ALL OF US SINCE 1951

Specifically, I suggest that for the first four years the tax returns be prepared under both the current America DEBT PREFERENCE TAX CODE, and the new EQUITY PREFERENCE TAX CODE.

The taxes due would then be as follows:

Year one: 75% of taxes due under old law.   25% under new law.
Year two: 50% of taxes due under each set of laws.
 Year three: 25% of taxes due under old law.   75% under new law.
Year four: 100% of taxes due under new law.

While this may sound complicated, it will be 'a piece of cake' for both governments and civilians.

By ending Democrats TAX THE RICH policy, America will return to the "Economic Reality" of Cleopatras era. Millions of America's families, and America's cities, states, counties and Federal Government, will all be able to climb out of debt.

TAX THE RICH Democrats are Public Enemy #1.

While at CCH & COMPUTAX decades ago, one accounting firm produced a 110-pound tax return for several hundred partners off of just one set of input forms. It was a giant real estate tax shelter with hundreds of investors. Why was it not taxed as a corporation?

Why does a two-investor corporation pay corporate income tax when a 250-partner real estate investor does not?

There are many skilled thinkers in and out of Washington eager to help solve our national mess. In just two years the IRS will know how low to set rates, or they could ask IBM to volunteer "Watson!"

DEMOCRATS OVERTAXED ALL OF US SINCE 1951

ENTREPRENEURIAL TAX NEEDS

"Entrepreneurs and their small enterprises are responsible for almost all the economic growth in the United States."
President Ronald Reagan

The founding principle of a TAX CODE is to produce revenue to pay the nation's bills, maintain an excellent credit rating, provide funds for national defense and advocate policies conducive to the raising of families that contribute to the needs of society in peace and at war.

The first English settlement was in Virginia in 1607. The Pilgrims arrived at Plymouth in New England in 1620. There was not a single home, store, office, trading post, or factory when they arrived.

Settlers knew that before anyone could live in a house, they had to build them. They also knew that before anyone could buy a product someone had to make it.

Both settlements organized themselves to meet the needs of families. They worked together to produce food, shelter, warmth and sustainability.

Our tax code needs to encourage that same kind of individual accomplishment, especially domestic self-sufficiency.

The first settlers founded America over 400 years ago. Everyone knew they had to work to produce homes, food, and heat to survive.

We salute Captain John Smith for setting the example in 1607 with his wise rule, 'No work, no food.' They did not tolerate free loaders or slackers.

They demonstrated that "Rights" carried "Responsibilities."

America needs the 'work ethic' of Captain Smith.

An EQUITY PREFERENCE TAX CODE will deliver many benefits to all Americans much as life was 400 years ago.

CHAPTER 4: DRAINING THE SWAMP

Mr. President, Nassau County, N.Y., elected a Democrat as chief executive in 2016.

She quickly replaced every Republican on the County payroll with a Democrat.

Follow her example.

Demand letters of resignation from every appointed Democrat in the Swamp. Your team can accept resignations at will to drain the swamp in an orderly fashion.

You cannot be accused of being 'unfair.'

You are merely doing to Democrats what Democrats first did to Republicans.

"Turnabout" has always been considered 'fair play.'

DEMOCRATS OVERTAXED ALL OF US SINCE 1951

CHAPTER 5: JOBS

Dear Mr. President,

President Obama's team once proclaimed that the millions of manufacturing jobs that left America "are never coming back."

That was a loud and clear public announcement of how totally incompetent he and his administration were.

(Or was he doing deliberate harm to America like doubling our National Debt while aiming for BANKRUPTCY?)

This is my position.

In 1984, when President Reagan was running for reelection, I found myself at a stop sign, surrounded by foreign cars.

I made this observation.

"I'm up to my Eyeballs in Imports."

Within a few days I finished writing a song with that title.

Then I put together a small and smart team of musical professionals and 'produced' a recording.

The team got airplay in 17 major music markets.

"Producer", Mister President, means I paid all the bills and took all the risk of making a profit or taking, for me, a giant loss.

My musical message is on the next page, but the page can't sing.

It just shows my simple storytelling lyrics.

DEMOCRATS OVERTAXED ALL OF US SINCE 1951

Unemployed worker
"I'm Up To My Eyeballs In Imports"
Autos and cameras and toys,
My TVs from Taiwan,
My shirts are from Hong Kong,
So how come, Boss, I'm unemployed.
I wrote once to President Reagan,
And asked him as nice as you please,
Is my unemployment,
What gives you enjoyment,
And why do we buy Japanese?
The President called me long distance,
Explaining me all o' that stuff

Reagan imitator
"Free trade and Tariffs and Balance of Payments
mean your life is bound to be tuff.
'Cause I'm up to my eyeballs in imports,
Autos and cameras and toys,
But Walter, my TVs from Taiwan,
my shirts are from Hong Kong,
buy I believe your taxes keep me employed.

Unemployed worker
I sent him a second short letter,
and tried hard to make it real clear.
I can't pay no taxes when I ain't a workin',
and imports don't pay taxes here.
The President called me to re-ply,

Reagan imitator
I see things in quite a new light.
If you're coming up short
I'll vote to tax imports
And be re-elected for life.

Duet:
We won't be Up To Our Eyeballs In Imports
Autos and cameras and toys.
Build more cars in Motown,
Pick up where we fell down
And we'll never be unemployed.
(Repeat and fade)

DEMOCRATS OVERTAXED ALL OF US SINCE 1951

My team did a great job.

They got my song air play in 17 major music markets.

For two days.

Foreign advertisers had a true story (Import don't pay taxes here) BLACKLISTED.

(Pushed off the radio play lists.)

Are there any patriotic recording artists in America? Call me. I'm almost 90 and need a little money to keep cheering for True Americans.

Courageous Republicans.

Chapter 6: IMMIGRATION

D. A. C. A. is President Obama's Trojan Horse

Obama's purpose was the same as the original: do fatal harm to the recipients.

President Obama encouraged an invasion by over 800,000 foreign forces. Was that #Treason?

History lesson: **Americans fought World War II to protect our nation from invasion by foreign forces.**

Germany, Japan and Italy wanted to invade America, own our resources, enjoy our standard of living and <u>enslave our children, our men and every American woman</u>.

DEMOCRATS OVERTAXED ALL OF US SINCE 1951

Over 16,000,000 Americans saw military service as they fought to save our nation.

Over 400,000 American servicepersons, male and female, died protecting us.

Those who served gave between 3 and 5 years of their lives, for a total loss of over 60,000,000-man years of their earnings.

Those who served lost 120 billion hours of income.

Because they saved America, history has named them "The Greatest Generation."

If we allow 800,000 invaders to stay, they could import millions more family members who never did a thing for America.

The illegals could dominate our native-born population and take control of America.

ACTION NEEDED:
We must return ALL illegal invaders to their homelands or other lands. Unharmed. Reunite illegal invaders in Mexico.

Their only loss is a few months of effort trying to break America's laws. Costs incurred should be a learning experience to the World: Do not waste your time and money breaking America's laws.

DEMOCRATS OVERTAXED ALL OF US SINCE 1951

May I propose a new immigration policy?

**1. Limit annual immigration to 0.1% of our current population.
2. Rebalance our population to the 1940 ethnic ratios of "The Greatest Generation."**

I'm old. I will be 91 before the 2020 Election.
But I have an excellent memory on many vital subjects.
Pearl Harbor is still vivid to me. I visited that shrine.
My brother was in the Navy during World War II.
I was in the Army during the Korean War.
911 is very vivid to me.
I have sold law reports and tax services in lower Manhattan, including the original World Trade Center Towers. I saw those buildings burn and collapse. I saw humans jump from 30, 50 or more floors up.

Many people from other nations want "Asylum" due to fears of their own nation. America's 13 original colonies faced fear of their masters, the Crown of Great Britain.
Foreign born people must do what our Founding Fathers did: Go fight for their own homeland's freedom. Deny them Asylum.

American soldiers should never fight and die to restore a nation whose people will not fight for their own freedom.

Mister President, I pray my "Immigration" view will guide your decisions.
Great Grandpa Kelly

CHAPTER 7. HELPING HAND TAX SHELTERS

Congress passed high tax rates for public grandstanding. Then they passed laws that only the rich profited from: Tax Shelters.

The following if from my 1988 book, AFTER BLACK MONDAY, (Out of print.)

"Past and present tax shelter laws destroyed manufacturing by making productive investments less attractive than tax sheltered investments that received preferential tax write-offs."

"Huge loans were the key, and write-offs added to the National debt. They enrich the rich, hold down working families and increase the National Debt. "Super Star" Helping Hands Tax Shelters could do better.

"The "Super Star" Tax Shelter plan would give a deduction to high income taxpayers to invest cash only, without debt, in urban renewal or rural housing projects and defer income taxes on the investment. They could also buy existing public housing and sell it to 'current residents only' at a super low interest rate.

"This plan will give pride of ownership to the occupants, and replace Section 8 Housing. Sports stars could replace the hated 'Projects.'
They could also invest in new housing to replace blight in cities like Detroit. New jobs will make up the tax loss. Owner occupied buildings experience lower crime rates and help build stronger families.

"Future payments from the buyers would produce a lasting cash flow to the "Super Star" beyond their normal peak earnings years. The athlete, artist or investor would have naming rights to the building or project. They would also gain personal satisfaction in lifting up dozens or hundreds of their fellow Americans.

DEMOCRATS OVERTAXED ALL OF US SINCE 1951

"By giving more people a stronger shot at home ownership, America will cultivate a happy and productive population, cut crime, strengthen families and reduce the national debt. A WIN-WIN-WIN-WIN plan. "

Mister President,

Your Secretary of the Treasury is a brilliant man. Challenge him to create a great solution to the need for affordable, owner occupied housing that does not drain our Treasury.

An investment variation could be created to finance "Starter housing."

I repeat, "Families are America's greatest need."

Great Grandpa Kelly

The End

DEMOCRATS OVERTAXED ALL OF US SINCE 1951

End note 1.

My role in launching America's first rockets.

In 1953 I was fresh out of the U.S. Army from the Korean War. My position was "a new hire" in the Linde Air Products Division of Union Carbide and Carbon Corporation research laboratory on Main Street in Speedway, Indiana. At age 23, I got the job because of knowledge of using a Slide rule for algebra, spherical geometry and spherical trigonometry.

Linde had invented a process of plating metals with a thin super hard coating of tungsten carbide, the hardest metal on our planet. The product was sold by the 0.001 (thousandths) of an inch thickness applied. Most applications used 0.006 (thousandths) of an inch thickness applied. That was polished by diamond faced buffing tools to extremely fine surfaces.

My job was estimating the cost of meeting a customer's needs and quoting a price for the service. Linde knew they had a great product. I was part of the team searching for a market. The Linde sales force was beating the bushes coast to coast in search of customers.

I conferred with sales reps by phone daily. Quotes were sent by mail.

One incoming caller said, "I need a quotation for ten thousand cubic feet of oxygen."

"That is not my department, but I'll find out and have him call you."

Before I found the right person, a second call came in.

"I'm sorry to bother you mister Kelly, but have I to change the order. I need a quotation on one hundred thousand cubic feet of oxygen."
(No one had ever called me 'Mister' before.)

"That's more interesting. I'll double my efforts to find him."

My time in the lab was only a few months, and I knew little about who did what. In half hour or so a third call came in.

"Mr. Kelly, I'm so sorry to bother you three times in one hour asking for a quotation, but I have to change the order again."

"What do you need?"

"I'm supervising a room full of Ph.D.'s in mathematics, and they can't agree on where to put the decimal point.

"Are we back to ten thousand cubic feet?" I asked.

"No. I need a million cubic feet."

"Wow. May I ask what you plan to do with all that oxygen?"

"We hope to fire some rockets," he replied.

"Way I ask where you're calling from?"

"I'm calling from a place no one has ever heard of and probably never will unless we succeed gloriously."

"And where might that be?" I asked.

"Cape Canaveral, Florida."

"Good luck. I will call World Headquarters in New York as soon as we hang up. Thanks for calling Linde Air."

The rest is history.

A few months later I was promoted to "Hired Inventor", given a raise and a private office. I was also given a white laboratory coat to wear at work to display my new and much appreciated elevated rank.

#

P.S.   Re: The man supervising a room full of PhDs in mathematics: Here is the reason they didn't know where to put the decimal point. They did not have PCs, but were using 12" long engineers slide rules.

The K&E shown below has 10 scales on each side, and could handle very advanced issues. It was my primary tool as a Union Carbide estimator.

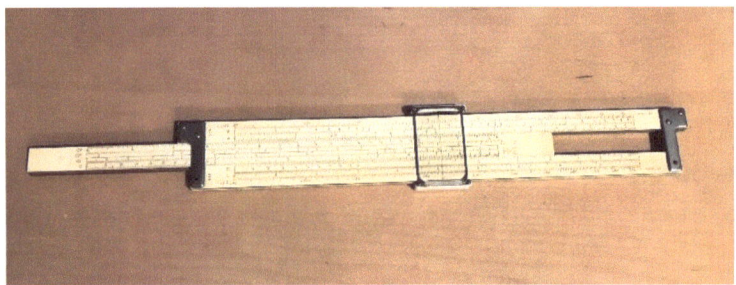

IBM introduced the first PC in August 1981. I bought my first one three days later.

#

End note 2.

My role in launching America's first passenger Jet Airliners.

After only six months at Linde I was eligible for one week of vacation. We drove to New York to see family and friends, some for the first time in three years.

First day back, I scanned my desktop mail box. The lab had been working with jet engine compressor blades for Pratt & Whitney and others for months. The copy of a quotation in my mail thrilled me. For a minute.

Then I took out my K&E slide rule and did some calculations. Next, I called the National Sales Manager for Flame-Plating.

"Carlson, I hope you didn't quote Pratt & Whitney yet."

"What's wrong?" He asked.

"That quote is based on doing the job in our laboratory. We can't do it here. It would take three hundred percent of our capacity even working 24/7. This is the market we have been dreaming about. But we need to think big.
"Carlson, jet engine impeller blades require careful handling, like eggs. One nick, scratch, crack, any bump that impacts the surfaces, their junk.
"Either Pratt & Whitney or Linde needs to buy land, build a factory, design and build special automated equipment. Then they must recruit, educate and train technicians.
"Carlson, that kind of estimating is beyond my skill level."

Carlson, the National Sales Manager, demanded my best estimate of rock bottom costs. I gave him what he needed, raw material only, emphasizing I could not quote on things beyond my experience.

DEMOCRATS OVERTAXED ALL OF US SINCE 1951

Fifteen months later a four engine Boeing 707 was America's first Jet passenger airliner. It was powered by four Pratt & Whitney Jet engines, each providing 10,000 pounds of thrust.

In one of life's delightful twists of fate, about 25 years later, a New York CPA customer advised how he had set up deferred compensation for Peter, Paul and Mary, who sang "I'm Leaving On A Jet Plane" in the 1950s.

#

www.ingramcontent.com/pod-product-compliance
Lightning Source LLC
Chambersburg PA
CBHW051209220526
45473CB00003B/968